World Traveler

Travel to
Japan

Matt Doeden

Lerner Publications ◆ Minneapolis

Content consultant: Hiromi Mizuno, Associate Professor of History at the University of Minnesota, Twin Cities

Lerner Publications Company
An imprint of Lerner Publishing Group, Inc.
241 First Avenue North
Minneapolis, MN 55401 USA

For reading levels and more information, look up this title
at www.lernerbooks.com.

Main body text set in Adrianna Regular.
Typeface provided by Chank.

Designer: Mary Ross

Library of Congress Cataloging-in-Publication Data

Names: Doeden, Matt, author.
Title: Travel to Japan / Matt Doeden.
Description: Minneapolis : Lerner Publications, [2022] | Series: Searchlight books: world traveler | Includes bibliographical references and index. | Audience: Ages 8–11 | Audience: Grades 2–3 | Summary: "Japan is an island nation in East Asia with a culture dating back thousands of years. Explore the mountains and coasts of Japan, discover its rich history, and tour modern-day Japan in this fun overview"— Provided by publisher.
Identifiers: LCCN 2021013004 (print) | LCCN 2021013005 (ebook) | ISBN 9781728441634 (lib. bdg.) | ISBN 9781728445014 (eb pdf)
Subjects: LCSH: Japan—Juvenile literature.
Classification: LCC DS806 .D635 2022 (print) | LCC DS806 (ebook) | DDC 952—dc23

LC record available at https://lccn.loc.gov/2021013004
LC ebook record available at https://lccn.loc.gov/2021013005

Manufactured in the United States of America
1-49918-49761-7/6/2021

Table of Contents

Chapter 1

GEOGRAPHY AND CLIMATE

The island nation of Japan rises out of the Pacific Ocean. Volcanoes and earthquakes sometimes reshape the land. Japan has towering mountains, open plains, long coasts, and rich valleys.

The Islands

Japan sits on the Japanese archipelago. This string of islands lies between the Sea of Okhotsk, the East China Sea, and the Philippine Sea. These seas are all part of the Pacific Ocean. Japan's four main islands, Hokkaido, Honshu, Shikoku, and Kyushu, are its largest and most populated. But the archipelago has almost seven thousand other islands. People live on many of these smaller islands.

Underwater volcanoes sometimes make new Japanese islands. In 2013, a new island emerged from an eruption near the Nishinoshima volcano.

Ishigaki, a small island in the southern part of the Japanese archipelago

Mountains

About 73 percent of Japan's land is mountainous. The islands are the tops of mountains that lie along Asia's continental shelf. Tectonic plates are large pieces of Earth's crust that shift and move. Most mountains in Japan formed when Earth's tectonic plates smashed into one another. These include the Hida Range and Akaishi Range in central Honshu.

Volcanoes formed other mountains. Mount Fuji stands 12,388 feet (3,776 m) tall. It is Japan's tallest peak. It is also an active volcano. Its last eruption ended in 1708.

Mount Fuji

Must-See Stop:
Chichibu 34 Kannon Temple Circuit

Nature blends with history along the Chichibu 34 Kannon Temple Circuit. This trek through the mountains of the Saitama Prefecture shows off Japan's natural beauty and its rich history. Visitors can see thirty-four historic temples set into the forest. Some date back hundreds of years. April is a perfect time to visit. Cherry blossoms are in bloom, setting a beautiful pink backdrop for the visit.

The city of Niigata sits along the Shinano River.

Lakes, Rivers, and the Coast

When rain falls on Japan's mountains, it runs down into a complex system of rivers and lakes. Mostly, Japan has fast-moving rivers. Hydroelectric dams along the rivers supply power to millions of people. The Shinano River is Japan's longest at 228 miles (367 km) long. Japan has several large lakes. Lake Biwa is its largest. This ancient lake has held water for more than four million years. It is up to 341 feet (104 m) deep.

Japan's coasts are home to most of its people. Beaches, large bays, and rocky islands dot the nation's long coastlines.

Climate

Japan's climate stretches from subarctic in the north to subtropical in the south. Most of the country has a temperate climate. Temperate climates have four seasons, with warm summers and cold winters.

Elevation has a big impact on climate. Japan's mountain ranges are cold. Many are snow-covered. Yearly snowmelts feed Japan's rushing rivers.

Mount Zaō becomes covered with juhyo, or snow monsters, in the winter months. The "monsters" are really snow-covered fir trees.

Chapter 2

HISTORY AND GOVERNMENT

People have been living on Japan's islands for at least thirty thousand years. The Jōmon period began around 10,500 BCE. The people were probably hunters and gatherers. Experts disagree about exactly when, but between 1000 BCE and 300 BCE, the Yayoi culture emerged. The Yayoi people were farmers. They grew rice and other crops.

Early Japan

People thrived in the Yayoi period. Japan was split into many kingdoms—as many as one hundred! The kingdoms battled for power. For more than 1,500 years, kingdoms and various governments rose and fell in Japan. Powerful warriors called samurai led armies into war. Eventually, warriors called daimyo helped to unify Japan under military control. In 1603, the Tokugawa, or Edo, period began. This time of peace and stability lasted more than 250 years.

A re-creation of what a Jōmon village may have looked like

The Battle of Sekigahara in 1600 led to the establishment of Tokugawa (military) control over Japan.

In 1868, the Meiji Restoration brought control of Japan back under Emperor Meiji. In the years that followed, Japan changed dramatically. The country's rulers pushed changes in an effort to defend Japan from foreign powers. As a result, Japan went from an isolated agricultural nation to a modernized, industrialized one open to foreign technology.

War and Disaster

Under Emperor Hirohito, Japan invaded Manchuria (part of modern-day China) in 1931 and China in 1937. During World War II (1939–1945), Japan allied with Germany and Italy to fight the Allies, led by Britain. In late 1941 Japan attacked Pearl Harbor, a US naval base in Hawaii, spurring the US to enter the war alongside the Allies. The fighting ended in 1945. That year, the US dropped atomic bombs on the Japanese cities of Hiroshima and Nagasaki,

HIROHITO LOOKS OVER JAPANESE SOLDIERS AROUND 1926.

and the Soviet Union, a group of republics that included Russia, entered the war on the Allies' side. The bombs, combined with air raids and new attacks, killed hundreds of thousands of civilians. But Japan recovered, becoming the world's second-largest economy by 1968.

Disaster struck again on March 11, 2011. An earthquake struck off the coast of Japan. The quake caused a tsunami. This large, powerful wave slammed into the coast of eastern Japan. It caused a deadly accident at the Fukushima Daiichi Nuclear Power Plant. Overall, nearly twenty thousand people died.

The Fukushima Daiichi Nuclear Power Plant

Prime Minister Yoshihide Suga speaks to the House of Representatives in 2021.

Government

After World War II, Japan changed from a military empire to a country with a pacifist, or peaceful, constitution. It became a strong democracy. Japan still has an emperor, but he plays only a symbolic role. The leader of the government is the prime minister. The nation's legislature makes the laws. It includes the House of Councilors and the House of Representatives. The Supreme Court is the highest court in Japan's judicial system.

Japan has forty-seven prefectures. These are similar to US states. Each prefecture has its own government.

Let's Celebrate:
Shōgatsu and Seijin no Hi

Shōgatsu is the Japanese celebration of a new year. Families clean their homes and get ready for a fresh start. On New Year's Eve, many celebrate with fireworks and go to Buddhist temples. The next day, millions flock to Shinto shrines to pray for a successful year. January 15 is Seijin no Hi. Everyone who turned twenty in the previous year celebrates coming of age, or becoming an adult.

A Buddhist temple

Chapter 3

CULTURE
AND PEOPLE

About 98 percent of Japan's people are of Japanese descent. People of Chinese and Korean descent are the next largest ethnic groups in Japan. They each make up about 0.5 percent of the nation's population. A wide mix of other ethnic groups including Filipino, Vietnamese, and Brazilians make up the remaining 1 percent.

THE FUSHIMI INARI TAISHA SHRINE IN KYOTO, JAPAN

Religion

Two main religions help shape Japan's unique culture. Shinto comes from ancient Japan. It is based on a belief in sacred spirits that take the form of the wind, rain, mountains, and other natural forces. Buddhism is based on the teachings of the Buddha, who lived in India around the sixth century BCE. The religion soon reached Japan. Many Japanese people identify as both Shintoist and Buddhist.

Language and Writing

Japanese is the main language of Japan. Several types, or dialects, of Japanese exist. But the most common is the Tokyo dialect. In some small pockets of Japan, people speak other languages. They include Ainu and the family of Ryukyuan languages.

Japanese writing uses a combination of characters. Kanji writing uses thousands of symbols to form words and ideas. Kana writing uses syllables to form word sounds. In modern times, letters from the Latin alphabet are sometimes added into Japanese writing.

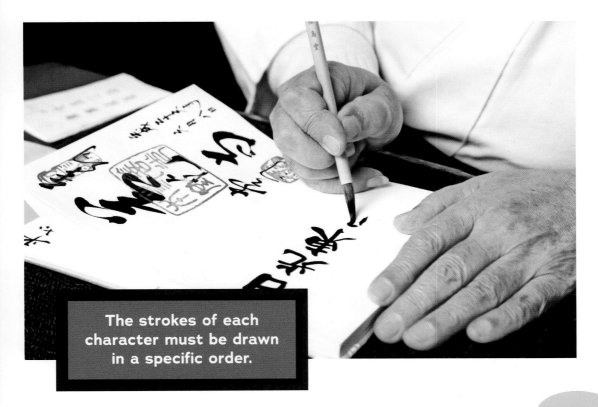

The strokes of each character must be drawn in a specific order.

Anmitsu might include jelly, pieces of fruit, sweet red bean paste, and more.

Food and Art

Japan's traditional cuisine is based on the country's resources. Rice is a staple of the Japanese diet. Flavorful soups, fish, and vegetables often go with the rice. One Japanese dessert is anmitsu, which is made with a jelly that comes from algae.

Japan has a strong art culture. Art forms traditional to Japan include kabuki theater, lacquerware, and a style of printing and painting called ukiyo-e. Another uniquely Japanese art form is origami, the art of folded paper. Origami artists create figures such as birds, turtles, and boats with careful folds. Japan also has a unique style of arranging flowers. It is called ikebana.

An origami crane

Let's Celebrate:
Children's Day

May 5 is Children's Day in Japan. On this special day, the nation celebrates children's growth and happiness. Many families hang koinobori, special carp-shaped streamers, to fly outside their windows. The carp symbolize a family's desire for their children to grow up brave and strong. Kids enjoy a day off of school to act in special plays and eat tasty kashiwa mochi, rice cakes wrapped in oak leaves.

Carp streamers for Children's Day

Chapter 4

LIFE IN JAPAN

Japan is home to more than 126 million people. Most of them live in cities. Tokyo is Japan's largest city. The Tokyo area is home to more than 37 million. Space in the city can be tight. Many Japanese people live in small houses or apartments. Overall, Japan is a healthy, thriving nation, with some of the highest life expectancies in the world.

Japan is a wealthy nation, home to the third-largest economy in the world. Technology is a big part of

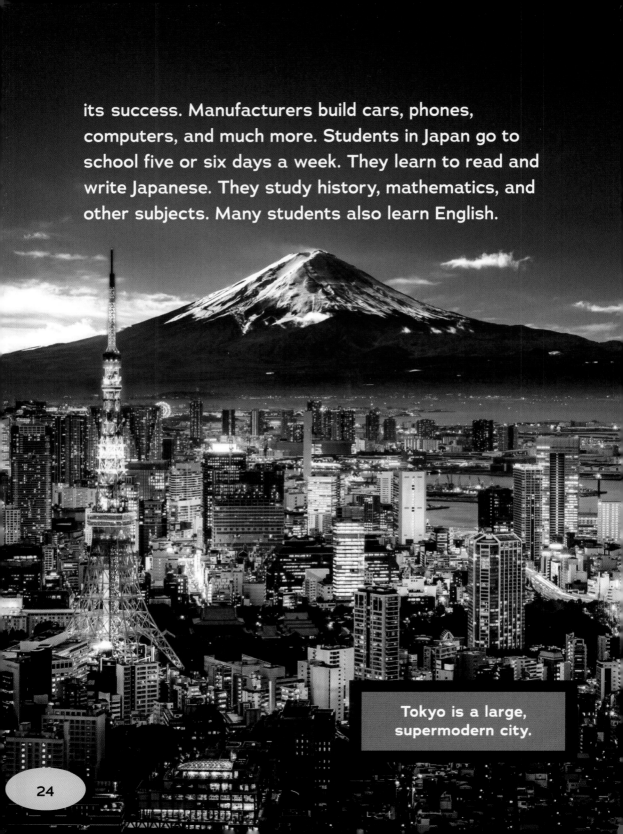

its success. Manufacturers build cars, phones, computers, and much more. Students in Japan go to school five or six days a week. They learn to read and write Japanese. They study history, mathematics, and other subjects. Many students also learn English.

Tokyo is a large, supermodern city.

Must-See Stop:
The Adachi Museum of Art

Japan is famous for its many art museums.
The Adachi Museum of Art in Shimane Prefecture
combines both traditional and modern Japanese
art with beautiful gardens. Adachi Zenko, the
museum's founder, believed viewing the natural
beauty of the gardens would add to the beauty
of the art they contain. Visitors can enjoy the
museum's gardens year-round.

future Challenges

Japan is a thriving nation. But it faces challenges in the future. Its population is aging. Young people are having fewer children. That could have a big impact on Japan's economy.

A Japanese family folds origami together.

Okinawa, Japan

Many people in Japan worry about climate change. Japan is an island nation. Climate change and rising sea levels could be a huge problem for coastal areas. Japan is working with nations around the world to fight this threat. They hope quick action will help keep Japan thriving.

Map and Key Facts

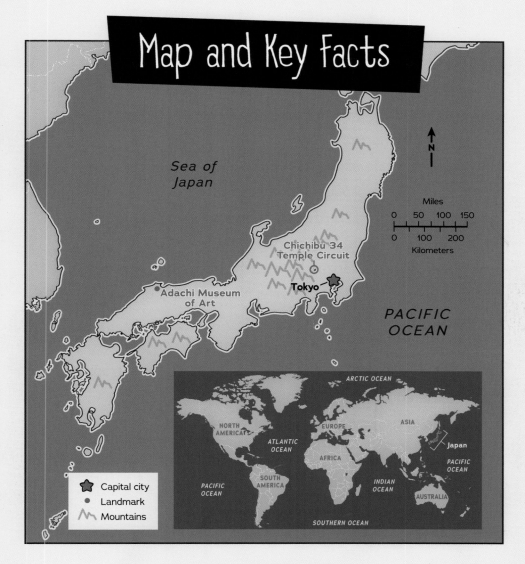

Sea of Japan

Chichibu 34 Temple Circuit

Tokyo

Adachi Museum of Art

PACIFIC OCEAN

Miles
0   50   100   150
0   100   200
Kilometers

N

ARCTIC OCEAN

NORTH AMERICA

EUROPE

ASIA

ATLANTIC OCEAN

Japan

PACIFIC OCEAN

AFRICA

PACIFIC OCEAN

SOUTH AMERICA

INDIAN OCEAN

AUSTRALIA

SOUTHERN OCEAN

★ Capital city
● Landmark
⋀⋀ Mountains

Flag of Japan

- **Continent: Asia**
- **Capital city: Tokyo**
- **Population: 126 million**
- **Languages: Japanese, Ryukyuan languages, Ainu, and others**

Glossary

archipelago: a chain of islands

continental shelf: the area around a large landmass that sits higher than the normal seafloor

elevation: distance above sea level

hydroelectric: the production of electricity from moving water

industrialized: characterized by advanced industry

legislature: the lawmaking branch of government

modernized: characterized by modern habits and technology

samurai: warriors from a powerful military class of Japanese society

subarctic: a cold climate that exists near Earth's poles

subtropical: a warm climate that exists near Earth's tropics, close to the equator

tsunami: a large, powerful wave, often caused by underwater earthquakes

Learn More

Explore Japan: Language
   https://web-japan.org/kidsweb/explore/language/index.html

Fehlen, Douglas J. *Explore Tokyo*. Mankato, MN: 12-Story Library, 2020.

Hansen, Grace. *Japan*. Minneapolis: Abdo Kids, 2020.

Kaminski, Leah. *Konichiwa, Japan*. Ann Arbor, MI: Cherry Lake, 2020.

National Geographic Kids: Japan
   https://kids.nationalgeographic.com/geography/countries/article
   /japan

Travel Japan
   https://www.japan.travel/en/

Index

Photo Acknowledgments

Image credits: Renata Barbarino/Shutterstock.com, p. 5; Sean Pavone/Shutterstock.com, p. 6; roadfair/Shutterstock.com, p. 7; Distinctive Shots/Shutterstock.com, p. 8; Chong Jian Ming/Shutterstock.com, p. 9; ZUN310/Shutterstock.com, p. 11; Wikimedia Commons PD, p. 12; CSU Archives/Everett/Alamy Stock Photo, p. 13; The Yomiuri Shimbun via AP Images, p. 14; Kyodo via AP Images, p. 15; Patrick Foto/Shutterstock.com, p. 16; Takashi Images/Shutterstock.com, p. 18; Aleksandar Todorovic/Shutterstock.com, p. 19; Tataya Kudo/Shutterstock.com, p. 20; mokokomo/Shutterstock.com, p. 21; Shin Okamoto/Getty Images, p. 22; yongyuan/Getty Images, p. 24; Tanya Jones/Shutterstock.com, p. 25; milatas/Shutterstock.com, p. 26–27; Lucas Shu/Shutterstock.com, p. 28; Laura Westlund/Independent Picture Service, p. 29.

Cover: ESB Professional/Shutterstock.com.